Friluftsliv

Everything You Need To Know About
The Nordic Lifestyle Of Friluftsliv

Sofie Bakken

Friluftsliv

Everything You Need To Know About The Nordic Lifestyle Of Friluftsliv

Sofie Bakken

BN Publishing

bnpublishing.com

ISBN: 9788443948561

© 2020 by Sofie Bakken

All rights reserved. No part of this publication may be reproduced, distributed, or transmitted in any form by any means, including photocopying, recording, or other electronic or mechanical methods, without the prior written permission of the publisher, except in the case of brief quotations embodied in critical reviews and certain other commercial uses permitted by copyright law.

Table of Content

Table of Content 5

Friluftsliv - Foreword 6

So, what is Friluftsliv? 7

What are the benefits of Friluftsliv? 12

Friluftsliv in 2020 14

It's all about the Money, Money, Money! 22

What are the differences between Friluftsliv and other popular lifestyle trends? 25

Friluftsliv in 2020 – there is a "But" 32

Is Friluftsliv the lifestyle choice for you? 35

Finally 39

Other Books by Sofie Bakken 40

Friluftsliv - Foreword

Just when you thought you had managed to get your tongue, and your head, around the words Hygge and Ikea's NORRÅKER and YNGVAR, all part of the range of flat pack furniture that we have come to love and hate in equal measure, we now have yet another Scandinavian word to struggle with, namely Friluftsliv.

So, what is Friluftsliv?

You will notice that I did not call it a "new" Scandinavian word, because it has actually been around since it was first used in a poem by Henrik Ibsen in 1859! He was a Norwegian playwright, poet and thinker, who coined the phrase when he was searching for meaning and purpose in his own life.

The poem is called "On the Heights" and the main character has chosen a life of freedom in the wilds, far away from the village of his birth.

Ibsen used the word "Friluftsliv" in the context of his thoughts, and more specifically in relation to his thoughts about life. He believed that the fundamental idea behind the philosophy is to experience the total connection and serenity that is possible when one is totally absorbed in nature. Not just surrounded by nature, but getting all one's spiritual, mental and physical needs met by Mother Nature.

What is really significant about this poem is *where* he wrote it. He was sitting on a small wooden stool, in front of a fire, inside a simple cottage somewhere in the wilderness of Norway.

It is not easy to find a precise definition for Friluftsliv because it is an all encompassing term for a simplistic lifestyle that embraces the complexities of that free life lived in simplicity.

In essence, Friluftsliv means to be close to nature, to develop the ability to co-operate with the natural world and to experience the joy of being in nature. It's more of a philosophy and way of life than an organised activity that just happens to take place outdoors.

By the way, the correct pronunciation of this word is *free-loofts-liv* and it literally means free *air life.*

In Scandinavia, the freedom to enjoy nature and connect with the countryside, is as fundamental as breathing, eating and drinking, and is deeply entrenched in the psyche of the people. In fact, it even encompasses their concept of spirituality and wholeness as a person.

Scandinavians are nature-loving people and it is easy to understand why. Being surrounded by outstanding natural beauty, gives them the opportunity to be immersed in the wonders of nature from birth to death. The fact that the weather is sometimes very hostile does not detract from the need to experience nature in all its forms. They say, "There is no such thing as bad weather, only bad clothing."So, there is no excuse for not getting out into nature every day of their lives.

Norway and Sweden, in particular, have vast, uninhabited areas of natural beauty. In addition to this, there is an unwritten law of "Allemansratten" (ones-right) that entitles anyone to access the land, even private property, provided that they do so for a limited time and treat the land with respect.

For most Norwegian or Norse people in general, friluftsliv is basically taking a walk in nature. This could also be a run if the person is adding a fitness element to it. People enjoy friluftsliv as a solitary pleasure, with friends as a social outing or in organised groups. It is something that they enjoy on a regular basis i.e. daily, with longer times spent outdoors in their free time, including weekends and holidays.

As I mentioned before, weather plays no part in the decision about whether to go out or not. Scandinavians merely dress appropriately, and use whatever equipment makes the outing more enjoyable. So, they will use skis, sleds, skates or snowshoes in the winter and enjoy cycling, rowing, swimming and walking in the warmer months.

There outdoor excursions can include pursuing hobbies such as photography and bird watching, foraging and fishing.

For many people it is the perfect place to practice Mindfulness or meditation, so it can also be a deep and spiritual experience. Breathing fresh air and clearing the mind of stress gives deeper meaning to friluftsliv.

What are the benefits of Friluftsliv?

1. Friluftsliv is free!
   All you need to do is go outside. Even in the big cities, parks and nature trails are not far away and open to everyone.
2. You don't need fancy or expensive equipment.
3. You don't need any instruction or a support group to accompany you. You can enjoy it alone or make it a social occasion.
4. You can enjoy friluftsliv whenever it suits you. There is no set time to start and there are no time limits on the duration of the experience. If one is enjoying the moment, then let it flow until it reaches a natural conclusion. No need to rush anywhere.

5. The physical and mental benefits from spending time in nature are well-documented. It's a great stress buster!

Friluftsliv in 2020

It is easy to find out more about the historical roots of Friluftsliv in Scandinavia, and also to appreciate how it has become engrained in the culture of those who live in northern climes. But, does it have any value for Scandinavians, or indeed the rest of us, in 2020?

We have the answers to almost all our questions, about life and how to live it, at our fingertips these days. However, we all seem to struggle with how to live a long and happy life in the twenty-first century, even with all the advances in science, technology, medicine etc. So, we are on a constant search for people and places that have achieved that goal. The fact that Scandinavia comes up in first place for happiness levels, as well as ranking the highest in the world for life expectancy, must mean that they are onto something.

Now, it's obviously not possible for us all to "up sticks" and move to the wilderness of Sweden or Norway. So, how can we learn from their lifestyles and practices and incorporate the benefits while continuing to live where we are, with all the stresses and strains of modern living? In other words, does this philosophy translate globally? Is it possible to enjoy friluftsliv on the streets of London or in the rainforest of Borneo?

Obviously, we all have valuable traditions and beliefs that we can adopt from our past. For example, natural remedies for illness, and recipes for homemade food that is nurturing and wholesome. However, it is interesting to investigate whether the philosophy of friluftsliv is one of the reasons why young Scandinavians are "living the good life".

So what does this philosophy look like in Scandinavia today? The truth is, many Nordic people are still enjoying the benefits of friluftliv today because these countries have embraced the modern world with all its mod cons, without allowing this important philosophy to be relegated to the history books.

At this point I should add that, not all young Scandinavians are totally committed to this philosophy and I will explain why later.

Here are some of the ways that friluftliv has been integrated into the lives of modern Scandinavians:

- **Education:**
  Children are taught the benefits of this lifestyle from birth. They see their parents practising it when they take babies out for walks in the fresh air no matter what the weather. They are fully informed of the benefits of spending time outside for their physical, mental and spiritual wellbeing, and they see the evidence all around them.

Over the last decade, many volunteer organisations, such as the Scouts, have taken the initiative to educate young people about the benefits of friluftsliv. This is now part of the policy for helping migrants, amongst others, to become familiar with the practice and to help them integrate into a new culture.

- **Flexible working hours:**
Daylight is in short supply for much of the year in the very far north of the world. For this reason, having flexible working hours enables workers to enjoy the outdoors when it is light, and then to do their work indoors when it is dark. This simple strategy gives workers the freedom to choose when to work. There is no reduction in productivity because workers feel respected and in a better frame of mind having had time to revitalize their minds and bodies when

they have been outdoors enjoying nature.

Flexible working hours also enable parents to be fully involved in all aspects of family life and helps to facilitate a happy family unit.

- **Company incentives:**

Among the many incentives that are available to Scandinavian workers, here are a few that make friluftsliv a lifestyle possibility:
- 90 minutes per week can be taken on a Wednesday for workers to enjoy friluftsliv.
- Meetings outside are encouraged. The benefits include new perspectives, inspiration and tranquillity.
- There are tax breaks for companies that facilitate friluftsliv. They can get this by offering incentives such as pay compensation for cycling or

walking to work, or subsidise gym memberships and the purchasing of sports equipment.

At this point, I would like to add some insights from my own experiences of living and working in one of the most significant countries in the First World. This country is situated in the northern hemisphere, although not as far north as Scandinavia. It experiences long, cold winters with occasional snow. For reasons I cannot explain, this country has chosen to pursue a philosophy that is totally opposite to that of friluftsliv. Here are some examples of what I mean:

- School children are discouraged from going outside at break time if there is a bit of drizzle and they are definitely not allowed out if there is a hint of ice or snow on the playground. Instead, they are kept

indoors and must entertain themselves with a collection of old toys from the "Wet Play" cupboard or watch inane videos. So, they spend that time cooped up, spreading germs and getting no exercise whatsoever.
- Parents clog up the roads and sidewalks with large 4x4 vehicles when they come to pick up their children and complain if their children are expected to stand outside for any length of time in cold, wet weather.
- Nobody expects the trains to work in autumn when there are leaves on the line and the mere mention of snow causes schools, airports, etc to close.
- The traditional shops on the high street are closing or moving to enormous malls. Children are encouraged to hold birthday parties in indoor entertainment centres

rather than parks and gardens. This all comes with hefty price tags.

And people wonder why depression is one of the major growing mental illnesses of 2020?

It's all about the Money, Money, Money!

As with most things in life these days, commercialism is the driving force. If it is possible to make money from people's chosen lifestyle, then somebody will find a way to do so. And so we see how people in some countries of the world have been lured away from living simply and in touch with nature. Many of them are not even aware that this manipulation has taken place. All they have to show for the pile of receipts is often a feeling of emptiness and loss.

Sadly, commercialism has taken advantage of the concept of friluftsliv in its birthplace as well as in other parts of the world. The fitness phenomenon has taken over the modern world, and whether it be indoors or out in the wilderness, people believe that if they have paid for the privilege, then it has got to be more effective.

So, having the best and most expensive equipment for performing exercise has become more important than getting outdoors to soak in the atmosphere and beauty of your natural surroundings. These days, exercising in nature is more about using the outdoors to test equipment and human resilience than for the mental, physical and spiritual benefits of spending time communing with nature.

And even in the natural places for exercising friluftsliv has become commercialised. You have to go to the "right" natural place, even if that means travelling long distances. Then you are enticed into buying or hiring expensive equipment and paying for expensive lessons!

It is not difficult to see that the original philosophy of friluftsliv has been corrupted slowly and surely around the world. In some cases, there is a slightly diluted version or it has been reduced to a merely superficial activity that is so far removed from the original idea of friluftsliv. Let me remind you of the basic philosophy:

Simply enjoy time spent connecting with nature. Fill your life, mind and soul with natural things and activities so that you can experience the benefits throughout your whole being.

What are the differences between Friluftsliv and other popular lifestyle trends?

Many of us now understand the concept of hygge and accept the commonsense idea of making ones home as cosy and relaxing for the usual inhabitants, as well as a very welcoming place for guests. We have seen this Danish lifestyle trend being incorporated into the decor of hotel chains and even the colours and textures of fabrics in business class on aeroplanes.

If you have not snuggled up against a woven, woollen cushion cover or been given a warm blanket to wrap around your shoulders in a trendy restaurant, then you can be forgiven for wondering what I am talking about.

Hygge is another ancient Scandinavian practice that became popular a few years ago in the world of interior design.

Like friluftsliv, hygge's natural origins are based in simplicity. It refers to a state or a moment of contentment and cosiness. When relaxing alone or with good company, in a cosy environment, lit only by candlelight, you would be well on your way to achieving "hygge" in your home. Add to that a homemade meal served in your handmade pottery bowls, and you would be able to tick all the hygge boxes.

And like friluftsliv, hygge has been commercialised to the maximum. Many of us are guilty of pursuing the dream of happiness and contentment by buying the trappings to try and replicate the Danish image of cosiness and contentment. Except, in all the hype, we might have missed the point. Authentic and original hygge and friluftsliv cannot be bought or manufactured.

The true essence of hygge can be experienced and enjoyed on a warm summer's evening, in the garden, around a long, wooden table with your family and friends. It's obviously easier to achieve hygge then, and it needs a bit more effort and imagination to achieve it on the coldest, darkest winter's day, but the feeling is the same.

By the same token, friluftsliv can be experienced indoors or outdoors – as long as the freshness of nature has been introduced into your life through the effort you have made to source the most natural products for your home and your menu. It will also be noticeable in your demeanour, the atmosphere in your home, how welcoming you are and how you live each and every day. It really is not something you can pretend to have or scene that can be set up like a stage set.

And what about friluftsliv and a wabi sabi lifestyle – are they compatible?

The concept of the perfect body, which we received from the ancient Greeks and Romans, has been taken to the extreme in the celebrity culture we now find ourselves living in. In fact, we have been told that everything must be "new" and "now" – except of course wine and steak, which should be aged to perfection!

So many people have angst about their looks, their bodies and I recently heard the term "house-shame" used by a U.K. based Kitchen Design Company! We are told that we must not accept the aging process in our bodies or our homes and we should certainly not be complacent about accepting flaws or signs of aging.

While recently researching design ideas for the old, stone cottage we are currently restoring in the mountains of Abruzzo, Italy, I came across a Belgian designer called Axel Vervoordt.

Axel has embraced the Japanese concept of wabi sabi in his design projects and he describes it like this:

"I find the spirit of things much more important than the look of things – I really don't mind if things are ugly. They have their own beauty, if only one looks hard enough." – Axel Vervoordt.

The Japanese phrase "wabi sabi" comprises two distinct ideas. – "wabi" means simplicity, and "sabi" alludes to the relentless passage of time and the marks it leaves. The philosophy of wabi sabi rejoices in the beauty that lies within imperfection. It is unhurried, tranquil, and respectful of faults and the signs of aging. It values authenticity above all else.

A quick look through the portfolio of Axel Vervoordt's work will show how he uses natural products and aged or flawed materials to create interiors of tranquillity and humility that cocoon the inhabitants of the room in a natural embrace. There are no frills or unnecessary glitz – only that which is found in nature.

And that is where the philosophies of friluftsliv and wabi sabi join in perfect harmony. While the superficial meaning of friluftsliv may be accepted as "being out in nature", we must remember that it encompasses all the aspects of the natural life cycle, the changing of the seasons and the working together with nature to provide everything for our bodies, minds and souls.

Wabi sabi is not a particularly cosy philosophy. Some might say that it can also appear a little harsh. But, like the natural world, it forces you to look carefully to see the beauty.

For example, the wrinkled, dry autumn leaves that are still clinging to the giant oak tree outside my window, do not look particularly beautiful when viewed individually. But, when you see them with the sunlight filtering through, the range of colours and shapes become something beautiful, although undeniably declaring the end of a season and death.

Friluftsliv in 2020 – there is a "But"

Believe it or not, after singing the praises of the friluftsliv philosophy, I have discovered a "But".

To be honest, the blame for the problem cannot be laid at the feet of the philosophy. The blame falls squarely on our obsession with being connected 24/7. Being able to mix technology with friluftsliv has created a deadly cocktail.

Because Scandinavia has achieved the status of being one of the most digitally sophisticated economies in the world, people can and need to access data and communication at any given time.

So, while you are out enjoying your friluftsliv, you will see people on their mobile phones as they walk or concluding mega deals while sitting on the veranda of their summer house.

Some young Norse men and women are finding it difficult to fit friluftsliv into their busy 21st Century schedules. Some people actually have to book the time in on their digital calendars.

With the help of the internet, the young Scandinavians are reconnecting with their innate desire to explore and are looking for distant destinations where they can spend their free time. They want to see new sights and meet new people and this is completely different to the uncomplicated origins of friluftsliv, when stepping outside your front door, was all that was needed.

Having instant gratification is important to the younger generation (and many of the oldies too), so the slow, gentle essence of friluftsliv is not necessarily compatible with their lifestyle choices. Some have even started experimenting with hallucinogenic drugs to speed up the process of relaxation when trying to fit a bit of friluftsliv into their busy lives.

And so, now they find themselves with the exact problem that the natural philosophy that they grew up with, could have solved for them. But, it seems they can't stop to smell the roses – or see the wood for the trees!

Is Friluftsliv the lifestyle choice for you?

We are now quite familiar with the philosophy that has made generations of Nordic people happy and healthy – both physically, mentally and spiritually resilient.

The ease and benefits of engaging with friluftsliv have been listed, and even if you do not live in northern Europe, it is possible to adopt this lifestyle. By simply taking that first step outside, finding a place in nature where you feel safe, tranquil and inspired, you will be on the way to achieving something that is exclusive and special to you.

These days, there is so little that is unique and individual. And if it is bespoke, then we fully anticipate that it is going to cost a considerable amount. Some of us even take pride in being able to afford such luxuries. I think it's called the "I'm worth it!" school of thought.

Friluftsliv, on the other hand, is totally your own creation. You can make it suit your preferences, your lifestyle, your body and your time. There is no right or wrong way to do it, no set of rules to obey or supreme master to follow.

You can make it as much of a solo spiritual experience as you like, or turn it into a perfect opportunity for making those social connections that we all need to keep us stimulated and connected.

You can do it sitting down, lying down, running or walking. You can enjoy friluftsliv while digging your vegetable garden or while picking and arranging a bunch of wildflowers in a favourite vase. You can do it while talking to a loved one on your phone, while soaking up the sun on your favourite beach.

Your home can reflect this philosophy by your choice and placement of aged, new, natural or handmade objects that have been selected for their authenticity and humility.

I am making it all sound so easy, aren't I?

"But, I'm doing all that and I just don't feel "it"," I hear you cry.

Friluftsliv is difficult easy. The oxymoron is intentional.

Whatever you do outdoors must be done with a sense of connectedness to the natural world around you. You have to be a mindful participant in the moment. Being a spectator of the beauty of nature is different from the all-encompassing feeling when you allow it to permeate your being and change you.

It is realising that nature is not going to change to fit in with you. You have to open yourself to an unconditional relationship with nature, in the same way that you need to in human relationships. You would not expect to really know someone after merely giving them a quick glance, would you?

You are not just an eco-tourist, who has paid a large amount of money for the opportunity to visit a new destination. Tourists feel that they have the right to complain about any discomfort or inconvenience that nature might cause to their enjoyment.

In friluftsliv, you engage with nature in humility and with a sense of awe, accepting whatever nature has on offer at that particular time. Yes, you need to open yourself to being mindful and meditative in order for friluftsliv to become a lifestyle rather than just a walk in the wild.

Finally

So, to end where I began – with the word "friluftsliv".

I am so glad that Ibsen gave this philosophy a name. Because, in spite of it being difficult to remember or pronounce, he made it accessible to the rest of us. If he had not named it as a "thing", we would have been wandering around in the forest without a trail of breadcrumbs to follow and we might have completely missed the opportunity to experience this wonderful lifestyle choice. Because it is so simple, it is hidden in plain sight. It's magical, yet down to earth. It's complicated and it is simplicity in essence. It's easy, yet difficult. It's free but it will bring benefits to your whole life that are worth their weight in gold.

Other Books by Sofie Bakken

www.ingramcontent.com/pod-product-compliance
Lightning Source LLC
LaVergne TN
LVHW010440070526
838199LV00066B/6103

9788439485619